The Basics of Bead Stringing

This book is the result of the collaborative effort of designers, artists and hobbyists who are in the profession of making jewelry. We have created this book in order to address the most common and popular questions of those who would like to begin designing and producing their own jewelry. We know that this book will be an asset to the novice beader as well as the teacher of beginners, because it provides the fundamentals as well as the latest knowledge of the art of bead stringing and beyond. Enjoy!

Contents

Beginning at the End:
The Classic Single-Strand Necklace

Materials

beads of your choice

carded nylon bead cord with wire needle attached

two small bead tips

one clasp with rings on both sides for at-taching to bead tips

one tube of cement or glue

thread cutters or scissors

chain nose pliers

bead board (optional)

Welcome!

The following lesson teaches how to begin and finish a necklace. Use these steps as a guideline for most necklaces while considering the particulars and intricacies of your own project. One challenge you may run into as a beginner is choosing the right size cord and clasp for your intended de-sign. (See pg. 49-61 at the back of this book for helpful hints on choosing the correct materials.)

1. *Lay out your beads in their intended design on a flat working surface that will hold your beads, such as a bead board or towel. Remove all beads from their temporary string.*

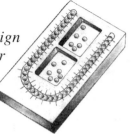

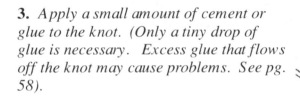

2. *Unwind your bead cord and remove the card. Pull the cord tight and tie a double overhand knot at the end opposite the needle. (An overhand knot is the same knot you use to start tying your shoe laces. To make it double, copy the drawing.)*

3. *Apply a small amount of cement or glue to the knot. (Only a tiny drop of glue is necessary. Excess glue that flows off the knot may cause problems. See pg. 58).*

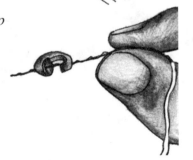

4. *String the needle through the top of one of the bead tips and pull the knot into the bead tip* 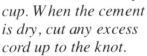 *cup. When the cement is dry, cut any excess cord up to the knot.*

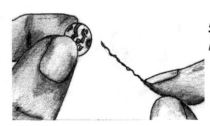

5 *Now simply string all your beads onto the cord.*

5

6. *To add the final bead tip, thread it as shown and pull it next to the beads. Try to remove any slack from your completed strand of beads by holding the needle end of your cord and allowing the beads to fall against the first bead tip.*

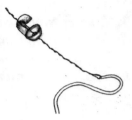

7. *Cut the excess bead cord but leave about four inches from the final bead tip.*

8. *Carefully untwist the bead cord into two strands and tie two overhand knots in opposite directions to secure the bead tip. Make sure the knots fit snuggly and are concealed in the bead tip cup.*

9. *Cement the knots and when dry cut off any excess cord.*

10. *To attach the clasp insert the hook of each bead tip through the loops of the clasp.*

11. *Using chain nose pliers, roll the end of each bead tip hook into the bead tip cup until it is closed. (See drawing) Make sure to close the bead tip by holding the end and curling it into the cup. This secures it and looks professional.*

 Correct

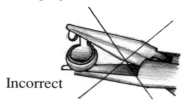 Incorrect

Using Bulk Thread and a Separate Needle

The lesson above used carded bead cord that included a needle. However you may simply buy nylon or silk twisted bead cord in bulk and thread on a separate needle. Make sure the eye of the needle will fit through your bead holes. You may also make a needle by stiffening one end with a small amount of glue. If you choose to thread a separate needle, the cord

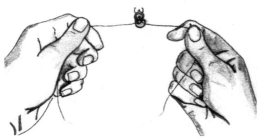 will be doubled so make sure both threads will fit comfortably through your beads. The advantage of using double thread is that the second bead tip can be tied securely with a double overhand knot after cutting off the needle. You do not need to untwist the cord like step 8 of this lesson.

Finishing Alternatives

Bead tips are not the only way to end a necklace, however they should be used when it is impossible to thread back through your beads because the drill holes are too small, or when the drill holes are so large that your knots will slip through. (See pg. 14-18 for alternative methods of ending your necklace.)

The Professional Edge:
The Knotted Necklace

The professional edge can be given to your necklace by knotting between each bead. Knotting adds beauty to your necklace and prevents the harmful rubbing of delicate beads such as pearls and gemstones. (Knotting also keeps your beads on their cord, rather than on the floor should your strand break while dancing!)

For this lesson use a pair of knotting tweezers and all of the same materials as lesson one. The tweezers are used to place your knots close to your beads. Use silk or nylon cord when you knot and pay close attention to the size of your bead holes. Some bead holes are too large or irregular to knot between and your beads may slide through the knots. (See pg. 49-51 for information on different cord options.)

Helpful Hints When Knotting:
- The key to knotting is to make each knot as uniform as you can and in the same direction. This prevents the beads from drawing up, appearing stiff, or hanging too loosely.

- Pull your knots taut but not so tightly that your necklace bunches up.

- Be aware that knotting can add about one to three inches to your design. (See appendix 2, pg.61).

- There is a special tool you may wish to use called a bead cord knotter which mimics the knotting process described in this lesson. (See pg. 59).

Select the largest size cord that will fit through the holes of your beads and make sure the cord is at least twice the desired finished length of your necklace.

1. *Attach your first bead tip as you did for the previous lesson and begin stringing all your beads without knotting. (Pre-stringing all your beads first will save the time of stringing each bead separately after each knot.)*

2. *Use a piece of tape at the end of the cord to keep your beads from slipping off the needle while knotting. Then let the beads fall down to the tape allowing room to make your first knot.*

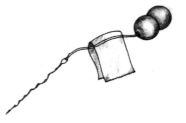

3. *Make a single over-hand knot as close as possible to the base of the bead tip. You can do this by wrapping the end of the cord around the four*

fingers of your left hand, and dropping the bead tip into the loop of the knot with your right hand. If you are having difficulties, look at the drawings and try to mimic exactly what you see.

9

4. *Put your knotting tweezers into the loop of the overhand knot and grip the cord with the tips of the tweezers as close as possible to the bead tip.*

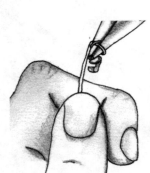

5. *Remove your left hand and pull the knot down the tips of the tweezers. Then carefully remove the tweezers and cinch the knot against the bead tip with your finger nail.*

6. *Slide the first bead up and repeat the knotting procedure. Continue sliding up new beads and tying knots after every bead, with a final knot retaining the last bead.*

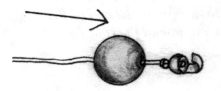

7. *End the necklace with a final bead tip and clasp as in the first lesson.(See pg. 5 and 6)*

The Professional Edge
Double Needle Method

If you find knotting difficult, you may wish to use double needles and thread. The extra thread also gives strength to your necklace.

1. *Cut off two strands of cord from the spool at least twice the length of the desired finished necklace.*

2. *Thread each strand with a separate needle, and tie them together with a double overhand knot at the end opposite the needles.*

3. *Thread both needles through a bead tip and pull the knot into the bead tip cup.*

Now you may use both hands to tie knots between your beads without having to use tweezers.

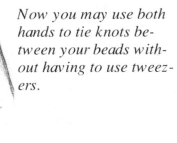

The Continuous Strand

Use this technique when you don't want to attach a clasp and your necklace is long enough to fit over your head.

1. *Put a piece of tape at the end of the bead cord opposite the needle to temporarily hold your beads. String the first three beads of your design in opposite order. The third bead of your design is strung first while the first bead of your design is strung third.*

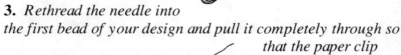

2. *Tie a knot about ¹/₂" away from the last bead you strung. Thread a paper clip or bent wire up to the knot. The clip must be removable.*

3. *Rethread the needle into the first bead of your design and pull it completely through so that the paper clip and knot are right up against the bead.*

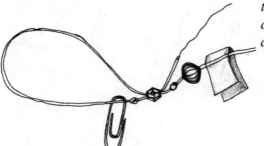

4. *Tie a knot between the first and second beads of your design, apply cement to the knot and run the needle through the second bead. Tie a knot between the second and third beads and then repeat the step tying a knot after the third bead. Cut the excess thread along with the tape from step 1. Cement all knots.*

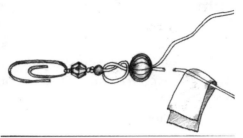

5. *Now string the rest of your beads onto the cord in normal order and knot between them. Leave the last three beads unknotted. (See pg. 9 for knotting instructions.)*

6. *Carefully remove the paper clip and thread the needle through the tiny loop it leaves. Pull the cord up to the last three unknotted beads.*

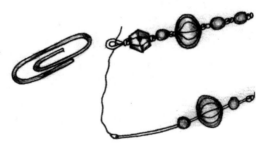

7. *Thread your needle through each of the unknotted beads and knot between them as in step four. Make sure to tie each knot by tying the knot around the cord as shown.*

8. *Cement all three knots and when dry, cut off excess cord.*

13

Finishing Your Necklace
Jump Rings, French Wire, and Clam Shells

The quality and professional appearance of your necklace depends on the way you attach your clasp to your bead cord. There are various endings and methods for finishing your necklace so once you have mastered using bead tips or continuous strands you may wish to experiment with the following styles:

Jump Rings:

1. *Put a piece of tape at the end of the cord opposite the needle and string the first two beads of your design in opposite order. (String the second bead and then the first.)*

2. *Thread the needle twice around a soldered (closed) jump ring and pull it towards your first two beads.*

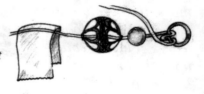

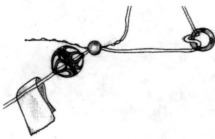

3. *Reinsert the needle into the first bead in the opposite direction of the initial threading.*

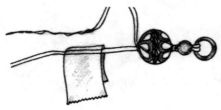

4. *Pull the thread completely through so that the jump ring lies snug against the bead. Tie a knot between the two beads.*

5 *Thread the needle through the second bead and tie another knot. Cut the excess cord.*

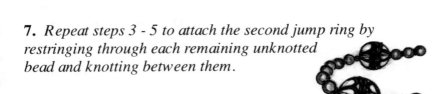

6. *Now string the rest of your beads onto the cord in normal order and knot between them. Leave the last two beads un- knot knotted. (See pg. 9 for knotting instructions).*

7. *Repeat steps 3 - 5 to attach the second jump ring by restringing through each remaining unknotted bead and knotting between them.*

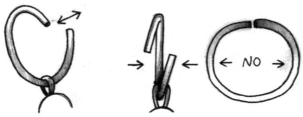

8. *Twist open the rings of a non soldered clasp with chain nose pliers like the drawing below and attach it to the jump rings.*

→ NO ←

Note: Use a soldered jump ring with a non soldered clasp. A jump ring that is not soldered may open causing the bead cord to slip off.

French Wire/Bullion:

1. *French wire, a hollow spring-like coil of fine wire is used to reinforce bead cord and is attached in practically the same manner as a jump ring. (See previous pg.)* With scissors, cut

a small piece of french wire approximately $^3/_8$" - $^1/_2$" (it is sold as one long coil) and string it onto the cord. (Put the needle through the hollow of the coil.) Now string on a clasp and two beads in reverse order of design.

2. *Re-thread the needle into the first bead like you did in step three for jump rings, but pull evenly on the thread so that the french wire will form a symmetrical loop*

around the clasp. Now proceed as you would with a jump ring.

Clam Shells/Knot Covers

1. *Tie a double overhand knot at the end of the cord and apply a small amount of cement. Thread the knot cover or clam shell up to the knot and cut the excess cord.*

2. *With chain nose pliers clamp the knot cover or clam shell around the knot so that it completely hides the knot.*

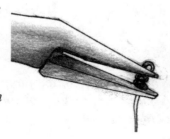

3. *Attach a clasp as you would with a bead tip. (See pg. 5-6.)*

Finishing Your Necklace
Crimp Beads with *Beadalon* ®

Crimp beads are used with soft, supple beading wire
(*Beadalon* ®) without having to knot or use a needle. Note:
Crimp beads cannot be used with nylon or silk twisted cord
because they may cut the cord.

1. *String a clasp and then a crimp bead
onto the Beadalon ® and slide them to
the end.*

2. *Thread the Beadalon ® back into
the crimp bead to form a loop around the clasp. Leave about
$^1/_2$" to $^3/_4$"
excess wire.*

3. *Hold the crimp bead with crimping pliers at a perpendicu-
lar angle while holding
both strands of
Beadalon ® together.
Slide the   crimp
bead towards the clasp.
You may also use regu-
lar chain nose pliers to
crimp. (See pg. 56).*

4. *Squeeze the pliers around the crimp bead to cinch it. This
takes some strength!*

5. *Thread your beads and
slide them over the excess
wire to lock the crimp bead in place.*

17

6. *Thread all your beads, another crimp bead and clasp attachment. Rethread the Beadalon ® into the last two or three beads and pull it tight against your clasp. Cinch the crimp bead with your pliers. Cut excess Beadalon. ®*

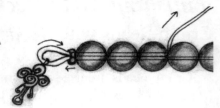

Note: If you are using other nylon twisted wire which kinks you may want to anchor your clasp to a board with a nail or tape in order to pull it taut.

How to Hide Crimp Beads with Clam Shells

Hiding a crimp bead with a clam shell/knot cover often gives a necklace a more professional look than just an exposed crimp bead. Try it!

1. *Thread a crimp bead onto the Beadalon ® and make a small loop like the previous lesson. Cinch the crimp bead at the end of the wire and cut excess cord.*

2. *Thread a clam shell/knot cover and close the shell around the crimp bead and loop. With a pair of chain nose pliers clamp the clam shell around the crimp bead. Repeat on the other end.*

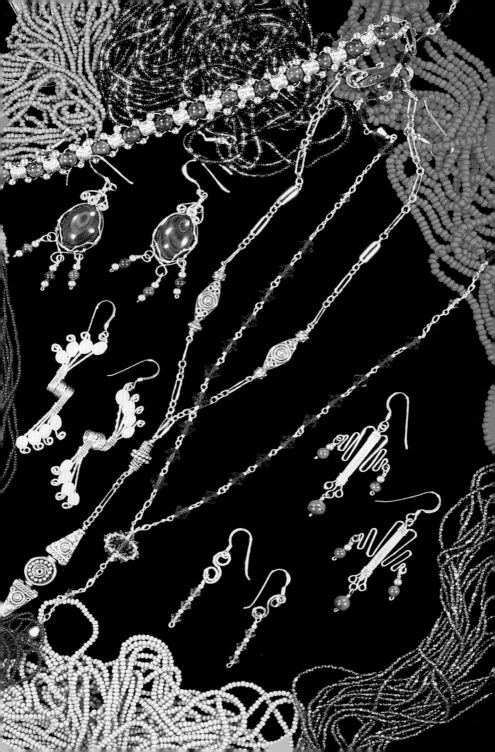

Using Wire and Pins
The Wrapped Wire Loop

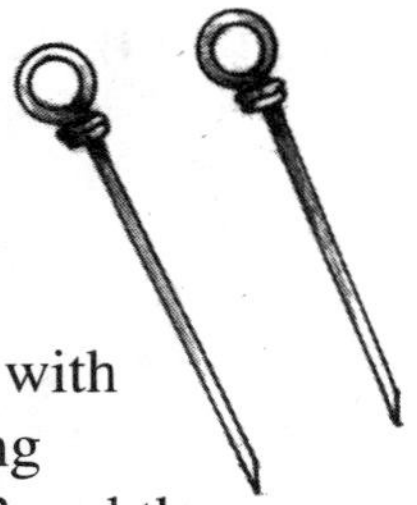

Use the technique on the following page with wire, head pins or eye pins to create connecting loops for your jewelry. (See pg. 22-33 and the photograph on the opposite page) Head and eye pins are very popular tools with beaders and are used to make earrings, rosary style necklaces, multistrand necklaces and much more. However, we recommend you use the wrapped wire loop instead of an eye pin. With time the loop of an eye pin may bend apart with stress causing your jewelry to fall apart. When you use a wrapped wire loop your jewelry will be secure.

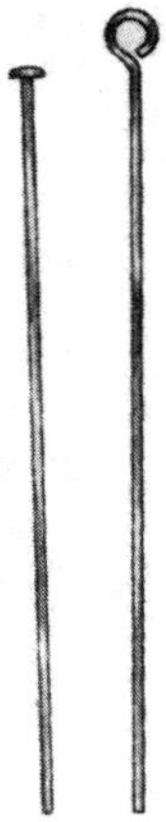

Essential Materials for Wire Working

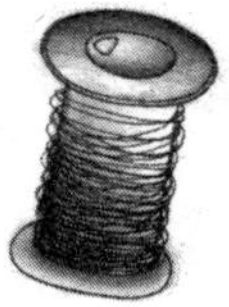

wire (see pg. 52)

wire cutters

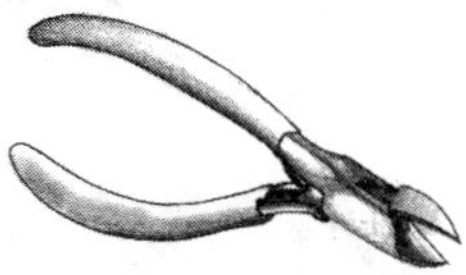

one pair of round nose pliers

two pairs of chain nose pliers

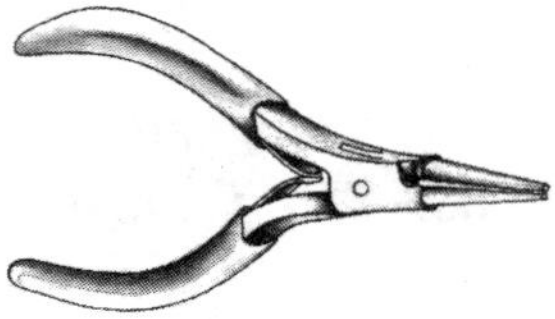

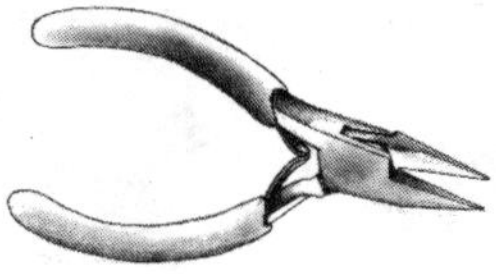

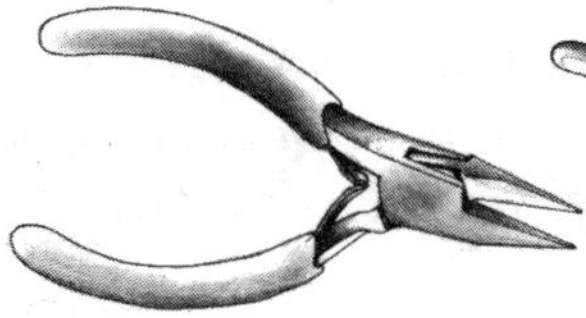

To Begin a Wrapped Wire Loop:

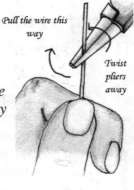

Pull the wire this way

Twist pliers away

1. *With your right hand (left if you are left handed) grip a strand of wire or pin with round nose pliers about 1/2" from the end. Make a loop by turning the wire away*

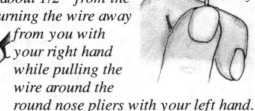

from you with your right hand while pulling the wire around the round nose pliers with your left hand.

Arrows indicate action already taken

2. *Use your thumbnail to straighten the loop.*

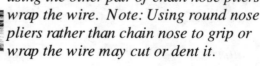

3. *Take one of your chain nose pliers and grip the loop while using the other pair of chain nose pliers to wrap the wire. Note: Using round nose pliers rather than chain nose to grip or wrap the wire may cut or dent it.*

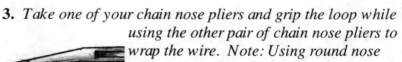

4. *Decide whether you want two, three or four coils. Two is most common. Remember to keep your coils consistent throughout. Clip off excess wire and with fine chain nose pliers flatten the cut wire so it will not scratch or snag.*

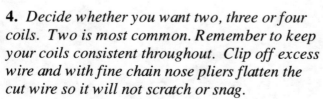

Using Wire and Pins
Basic Drop Earrings or Dangles

1. *Thread all beads onto a head pin.*

2. *Make a wrapped wire loop at the end of the head pin to secure the*

beads. (See previous page). You may connect the ear-wire while making the loop or connect it later by opening the earwire ring like the rings of a non-soldered clasp as shown on pg. 15.

You can use this same technique to create dangles for your necklaces! Follow the lesson above but instead of attaching the earhook, complete the wrapped wire loop and thread the dangle while you are threading beads onto bead cord, *Beadalon* ® leather or any stringing material.

Using Wire and Pins
Single Wire Loop Earrings

Many beaders choose to make earrings or dangles with a single wire loop rather than a wrapped loop. The single loop is less reliable than the wrapped.

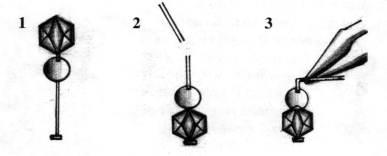

1. *Thread your beads onto a headpin.*

2. *Cut the wire about 1/3" from the beads or enough to make a loop.*

3. *With your chain nose pliers bend the wire at a 90 degree angle.*

4. *Holding the wire with chain nose pliers in one hand grip the end of the bent wire with round nose pliers and turn the wire into a loop. Attach an earhook while making the loop.*

Using Wire and Pins

Multistrand Necklaces

The key to working with multistrand necklaces is to create several single strand necklaces and to hide the ends when you attach them. This can be done with cones and the wrapped wire loop technique. (See pg. 22 for looping technique and pg. 53. for cones.) Although some beaders use eye pins to attach their single strands we recommend that you use wrapped wire loops which will hold the heavier strands secure.

Finishing With Cones

1. *Using the wrapped wire loop technique on pg. 22, make two separate loops out of wire leaving enough room to add cones, and another wrapped wire loop at the opposite end.*

2a. *Make two or more single strand necklaces using bead cord or Beadalon. ® Finish the strands and connect them to the newly created wrapped wire loops.*

2b. *As an alternative you may wish to leave your single strands finished just with a double overhand knot and enough cord at the ends to tie them to the wrapped wire loops. Use overhand knots to tie the strands and cement the knots secure.*

3. *Place a cone over the wire to hide the ends and wrapped wire loop. Make another wrapped wire loop at the top of the cone to secure it. While making the loop, attach a clasp.*

Finishing a Multistrand Necklace with a Multistrand Clasp:

1. *Multistrand necklaces may also be connected with a two or more ringed clasp. (See above) Attach your single strands to the rings of the clasp using any of the various finishing ends. (See pg. 53-54). You may also wish to thread separator bars throughout your strand to separate the strands from each other. There is no set formula for get-ting your strands to align with separator bars. Don't be surprised if you must add or subtract beads to allow your strands to hang evenly staggered.*

Using Wire and Pins
Intermittent Multistrand Necklaces

You may vary the number of strands in a necklace from one strand to as many as you desire by simply threading several cords into a single bead.

1. *Choose the greatest amount of strands you wish to have in your necklace and start your necklace with that number of nylon bead cord strands and needles. Take the loose strands and tie the ends to a wrapped*

wire loop, or finish by tying the ends together and clamping on one clamshell. Begin threading each needle into one bead.

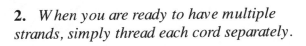

2. *When you are ready to have multiple strands, simply thread each cord separately.*

3. *To bring the necklace back to a single strand, thread each needle back into one bead. You can continue changing the number of strands in this manner.*

Using Wire and Pins

The Wrapped Wire Loop Necklace or Rosary Technique

Materials

beads of your choice

one pair of round nose pliers (essential)

two pairs of chain nose pliers

wire cutters

wire of appropriate gauge (Ga.) for beads between 20-26 Ga. See pg. 52

open link style chain (optional)

clasp (optional)

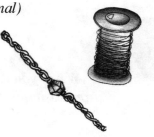

1. *Start with about 18" of wire. This length will give you something to hold on to and will cut down your waste. Make a wrapped wire loop at one end. (See page 22).*

2. *Add a bead to the wire and make another wrapped loop at the other end but this time hold the loop with chain nose pliers and wrap the wire with your hands. We have found that it is best to start the loop as close to the bead as possible.*

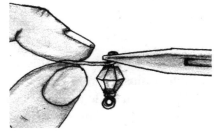

3. *Cut the excess wire and use chain nose pliers to tighten or flatten the coil. You may also have to use a flat needle file to smooth the rough edge of the wire. Note: To avoid this use flush cutters. (See pg. 57).*

4. *Make another wrapped wire loop with the cut wire. While making the loop, connect it to the first loop, or add a soldered jump ring between the loops for a looser joint. (Occasionally the loops may catch with one another. Using chain, jumprings or attachments takes care of this problem.)*

5. *Continue making links until you have reached the desired length. Wire loops are excellent for attaching chain, fancy connectors or clasps. Just connect the loops to chain links or soldered jump rings. To finish the necklace either add a clasp or make it continuous by connecting the loops at the end.*

Using Wire and Pins
Memory Wire

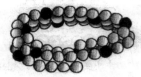

Memory wire is a flexible coil wire
which comes in preformed bracelet, necklace and ring shapes
and accepts a wide range of bead sizes.   Memory wire is
made out of hardened steel wire and unfortunately requires the
use of industrial strength cutters and pliers.

1. *You may finish the ends of memory wire
in one of three ways. A common approach
is to apply glue to a half-drilled bead using a*

*precision applicator, and then at-
tach it to the end of the memory
wire.*

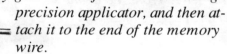

2. *Simply string your beads and attach another half drilled
bead at the other end. Note that the ends of memory wire do
not attach with a clasp.*

Other Options
1. *With heavy duty pliers bend the ends of the memory wire
into small loops. You may wish to
end your necklace, bracelet or ring
this way. Or you may wish to go on
to step 2.*

2.   *Thread a clam shell and clamp it over the bent loop.*
*Then clip off the ring
of the clam shell. In*

*this way the bent wire
acts like a knot.*

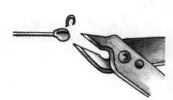

Using Wire and Pins
Wire Wrapping

Wire wrapping is a beautiful way to create your own intricate settings for cabochons, faceted stones, or anything you would like to accent with wire. Think of wire wrapping as sculpting with wire and pliers. It is an art which requires a great amount of improvisation and creativity. As a beginner, we suggest you wrap a large, flat, symmetrical stone such as a cabochon, rather than a faceted or odd sided stone.

Use 20 Ga. square wire rather than round which cannot grip the stone, two pairs of chain nose pliers, wire cutters, tape and a razor blade to separate bound wires. Round nose pliers are also useful for filigree and making loops.

1. *Make a sketch of your design and decide how many strands of 20 GA. square wire you would like to use. Generally an odd number of strands such as three or five works best. This lesson will use five strands.*

2. *Measure the circumference of the stone by rolling it along a ruler.*
Add three to four inches to that number and cut all the strands of wire at that length.

3. *Line up the wires and temporarily bind them at the ends with transparent tape.*

4. *Next you need to bind the strands with additional wire. Take into consideration the placement of the bindings. They must hold the wires together and should be decorative. Mark the locations of bindings with a black marker. (These markings can be buffed off later.)*

5. *Cut about three inches of 20 GA. square or half round wire flush and with your chain nose pliers bend one end of the wire to begin the binding. (Bend the wire along its natural bend.)*

6. *Now wrap the binding wire around your strands with your hands. Keep the strands lined up next to each other and the binding wire flat against the strands. Be careful not to twist the binding wire. Start and end your binding on the back side of the strands. (The side which will face down against the stone) Cut all excess binding wire.*

7. *Repeat the bindings where desired, (we chose to bind in four areas) and don't make them excessively tight. The strands must be able to slide through the bindings. Flatten the strands with your hands and remove the transparent tape.*

8. *With a razor blade separate the out-side strands and insert chain nose pliers to slightly pull the strands out of the binding. Form designs that will hold your stone.*

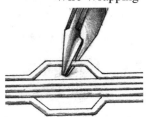

9. *Now mold the strands around your stone beginning from the bottom up. The wire will bend and is malleable. Remember which sides of the strands are to face the stone.*

10. *Remove the strands from the stone and grip them with one pair of chain nose pliers. With another pair of chain or flat nose pliers turn the separated wire in so that it will grip around the stone.*

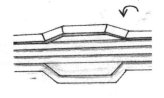

11. *At this point become the sculptor. Sculpt the strands around the stone with your hands and chain nose pliers so that they all end up at the top. Make sure the strands are tight and secure the stone on both sides.*

12. *Remember you need to end the wrap with loops on top so that you may attach the stone to a chain for a necklace. With the central strands and round nose pliers make wrapped wire loops. (See page 22) Attach all the strands at the top by wrapping them around the central strands. Cut the ends or make them into filigree using round nose pliers.*

Using Wire and Pins
Twisting Wire With a Pin Vise

The art of wire wrapping can be augmented by simply twisting wire strands in a pin vise and using them in place of straight wire. The pin vise is a handheld tool which comes with one or two double sided collets that grip the wire so you are able to twist the strands.

1. *Cut a strand of square gauge wire with wire cutters and attach them to the collets (grips) of the pin vise.*

2. *With chain or flat nose pliers grip the wire and begin twisting the pin vise with your other hand. Twist tightly and consistently.*

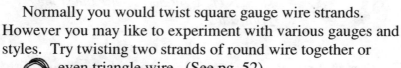

Normally you would twist square gauge wire strands. However you may like to experiment with various gauges and styles. Try twisting two strands of round wire together or even triangle wire. (See pg. 52)

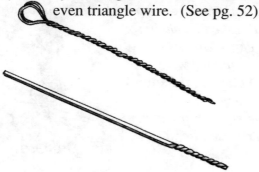

Hat and Stick Pins
A Quick Victorian Project

Hat and stick pins are commonly sold where clasps and findings are found. Clutches are sold separately.

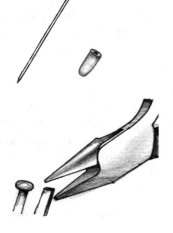

1 *Use a 6 inch hat pin or 3 inch stick pin with clutch. If the pin does not have a head use pliers to gently squeeze the blunt tip of the pin (not the point) until it is flat. This will secure the top beads.*

2 *String on your beads preferably with the larger beads at the head and smaller beads at the bottom. Secure them in place with a crimp bead or by applying glue with a precision applicator. Use chain nose pliers to cinch the crimp bead. Using a crimp bead is generally less attractive then using glue.*

3 *Attach a clutch for a quick finished project.*

Using Leather or Satin Cord
Knotting Techniques

Working with thick cord is ideal when you wish to hang large beads or amulets with knots. Often simple well placed overhand knots next to beads or amulets make all the difference when using leather or satin cord. Most beaders are sparse with beads when they use thicker cord so that the leather or satin and central amulet are all that is required.

Larks Knot
Use a larks knot when the amulet you are using can not be strung on the leather cord but can be hung. Donut shaped stones are most commonly hung with a larks knot.

Adjustable Slide Knot

Use this knot to finish your leather necklaces or bracelets. These knots can be adjusted next to central beads such as this bracelet.

Tie the right end around the left strand and the left end around the right strand. You may now adjust the necklace or bracelet to the size you wish. This is especially good for pulling necklaces over the head or bracelets through the hand.

Using Leather or Satin Cord
Finishing with Wire (Tracy's Clasp)

Here is a handy way to make a loop at the end of leather or satin cord in order to attach clasps and findings.

1. *Make a Z shape out of 24 or 26 Ga. wire as shown in the diagram.*

2. *Bend the end of your leather cord into a loop and enclose a jump ring. (Illustrations do not show jumpring). Crease the leather loop with your thumbnail. Place the wire over the end of you leather cord as shown and wrap the longer end several times around the cord. Make sure the coils are tight and consistent.*

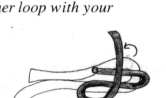

3. *Pull the wire as indicated in the diagram so that the coils are tight.*

PULL THIS WIRE ←

4. *Next pull tightly on the other side of the wire as shown in order to pull in excess wire. You want a neat attractive coil at the end of your leather. When you have pulled the wire as far as it will go, cut off the excess.*

PULL THIS WIRE ↓

5. *Cut off excess leather. Attach a clasp to your jump ring if needed. Make sure the jump ring is held tightly by the leather loop. If the ring slips it may catch in hair.*

Seed Beads/Rocailles
Daisy Chains

The small size of seed beads or rocailles allow the beader to create intricate designs, incorporating multiple threadings, weaving and stitching techniques as well as embroidery. These small glass beads originated in 15th century Europe and are made today in the Czech Republic, France, India and Japan in sizes ranging from 1mm to 5mm in diameter.

This book explains three popular techniques using seed beads in levels of progressive difficulty. We recommend starting with size 11 seed beads for all three projects. Use a very thin thread such as *Nymo* with English beading needles when stitching or weaving. For such simple techniques such as daisy chains use thin nylon cord and try substituting small gemstone beads for a different, elegant look. Always make sure to pull tightly when stringing to prevent sagging and holes. Be aware that *Nymo* thread needs several knots to hold bead tips because it is so thin.

1. *Using thin nylon cord size 1, finish one end with a clasp. (See pg. 49) String 5 petal beads and one center bead for a total of 6 beads.*

2. *Re-thread the needle back through the first "petal" bead to create half a flower.*

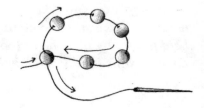

3. *String 3 more "petal" beads and thread the needle into the 5th "petal" bead creating a daisy.*

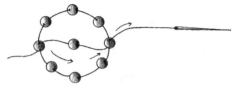

4. *To connect your daisies follow the pattern below. End with a clasp as in lesson one, pg. 5-7.*

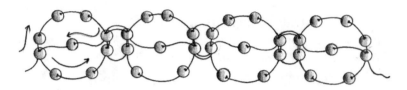

Adjusting for Bead Size

1. *This is just a variation of the daisy chain to allow for a larger center. String 7 size 11 seed beads for the "petals" with a 6mm round bead as the center. Re-thread the needle into the first "petal" bead.*

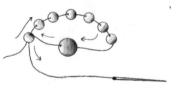

2. *String five more "petal" beads and rethread the needle into the 7th "petal" bead.*

A Helpful Hint

1. When seed beads are sold pre-strung on temporary cord, you can quickly thread these beads onto your bead cord by threading your nee-  dle through the pre-strung beads. The bead holes must be large enough and the pattern sold should be the pattern you desire. This tip saves the agonizing restringing of hundreds of tiny beads.

Seed Beads/Rocailles
Brick Stitch Earrings

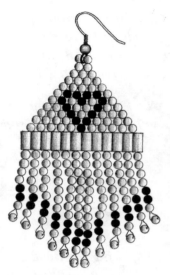

For most seed bead jewelry, once you have learned a stitch, new designs are eminent. These popular earrings consist of one row of inter-locking tube beads or bugle beads connected to a brick stitch triangle and loop of seed beads with a heart design. Keep in mind that a pattern such as this heart pattern needs a center point which means you should start your designs with an even number of rows. This lesson shows twelve. It is useful to lay out your design on graph paper first to get your bearings.

1. *Unwind about 4 feet of thread and work directly off of the spool. Use an even number of tube beads and form one interlocking row by following the diagram. Thread and connect each bead one at a time.*

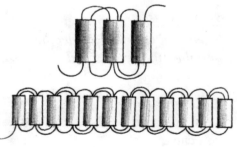

2. *Using size 11 seed beads, create a triangle in brick stitch following the diagram on the next page. You are starting with the thread from the last bugle bead and stringing it through a bead making a loop between the threads that attach the bugle beads. Each row will decrease by one bead.*

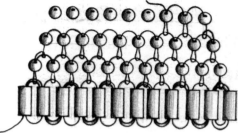

For the first bead in each new row, thread around the loop and then up through the bead as shown.

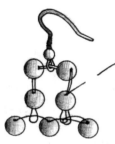

(This step will hide thread from showing at the outside of the earring.)

3. *When the row of your triangle reaches two beads, thread two more beads and an earhook to create a loop. Reinforce this loop four times by re-threading through several beads and tying square knots. This loop should be strong because it has the most strain and pull from the earwire.*

4. *To make the fringe decide on a style and design from this diagram or your own.*

5. *Unwind and cut about three feet of thread from the spool that is still attached to the bugle beads. Re-thread the needle.*

6. *Thread the beads as shown and bring the thread back up through the beads, and the bugle bead.*

7. *Each bugle bead can have a fringe attached to it. Knot the last fringe securely and discretely cut off excess thread.*

Seed Beads/Rocailles
The Peyote Stitch/Gourd Stitch

See photograph
after this lesson.

Materials

Japanese made seed beads

Nymo beading thread size A or B

English beading needles size 10-12

*white three-ply rope from an upholstery store
or any round base to use as a form*

thread cutters

tape to temporarily seal rope

Peyote stitch is derived from the method Native Americans use to cover items for religious ceremonies. For this stitch and other similar stitches it is best to use Japanese made seed beads which are the most uniform in size. The thread and needle must be very thin so that it can be rethread many times through each bead. The stitch is worked around a form which may or may not be permanent. A white three-ply rope is most commonly used as a form for peyote stitch necklaces because it is soft and pliable. Some beaders may use a wooden dowel or pencil as a temporary form that is removed to leave a hollow necklace. They find this easier than using a permanent form. The following lesson explains how to make a peyote stitch necklace but you can apply the same technique to make various decorative coverings. Have patience with this stitch for it takes time to master but will give you the basics of seed bead stitching.

1. *If you are using a rope, wrap tape around the ends to prevent fraying. Start the stitch about three inches from the end of the rope or other form. Thread the Nymo with a needle and enough seed beads to wrap around the rope or form. Use an uneven number to maintain symmetry. Do not work directly off the spool.*

2. *Thread the needle back into the beads to form a circle around the rope that is reinforced by the double threading. Tie a square knot to secure the circle.*

3. *Thread the needle through the first bead next to the knot and then thread on a new bead. Thread the needle through the third bead next to the knot.*

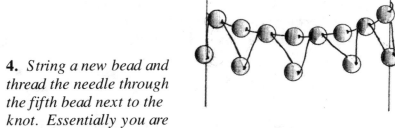

4. *String a new bead and thread the needle through the fifth bead next to the knot. Essentially you are threading into every other bead while adding a new bead.*

5. *When you have finished threading through the first row of beads, thread through the first bead again so that you can drop down as shown and be in position to start the second row. This step is very important. So don't skip it.*

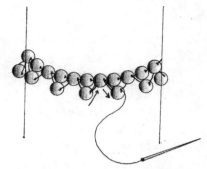

6. *To complete the second row you will notice a staggering pattern. The newly threaded beads will be lower than the first row. Thread between the staggered beads to fill in the second row. These first few rows can be strung loosely. When you reach the fourth row pull the stitch together. You may also notice that at first your beads flair out. Don't worry, as you stitch your necklace will become cylindrical.*

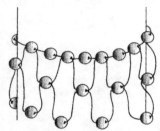

7. *Repeat the peyote stitch to the required length and make sure to leave about three inches of rope at the end.*

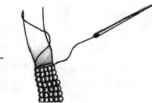

8. *If you choose to keep the rope, go back through several rows of your necklace and sew the beads onto the rope. Otherwise carefully remove the pattern from the temporary form with the spool still attached.*

9. *Now you need to close the ends of your necklace by tapering the stitch. If you are using rope cut it 1/4" past the beading. Continue the stitch but skip one bead every other stitch as needed and close the stitch around the end of the rope.*

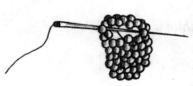

11. *Tie a square knot after your last stitch and re-thread through several other beads tying square knots to secure the stitch.*

Attaching a Clasp

- Ending a peyote stitch necklace relies on your personal preference and imagination. Some beaders end their necklaces with a bead tip and clasp. Leave a tail of Nymo thread at each end, thread on a bead tip and tie several overhand knots (see pg. 6) to secure the tip. Apply glue and attach a clasp as in lesson one.

- Other beaders create a loop of seed beads on one end which attaches to a sewing button on the other end.

- You may wish to end the necklace like a multistrand by attaching the *Nymo* thread to a wire wrapped loop and cone. (See pg. 22 and 25-26.) For this technique your peyote stitch should be narrow so that the cone will fit over the stitch. It is wise to glue the cone before placing it on your rope.

Tapering with
Buttonhole

Multistrand
Wirewrap

Seed Beads/Rocailles
Attaching New Thread

The intricacy of brick and peyote stitch often requires more thread than what you originally cut off the spool. Take care to attach the new thread discretely and securely. Add new thread when you have three to four inches of your first thread remaining.

1. *Thread a new needle with the new thread. Tie a knot at the end. (Leave the old needle on the existing thread.)*

2. *Add cement to the knot and cut off any excess cord.*

3. *Bring the new needle and thread through the last three or four beads of the project so that it mimics the path of the old thread. Tie the new and old thread with a square knot and add cement or glue.*

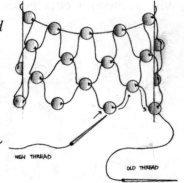

NEW THREAD

OLD THREAD

4. *Begin threading with both needles and pull the square knot snug against the beads. After threading three or four more beads cut off the old thread discretely.*

Materials and Tools

Bead Cord

There are so many kinds of bead cord available. When selecting the right cord for your necklace choose the heaviest cord that will pass through the smallest holes of your beads without fraying.   For most of the lessons in this book we recommend nylon cord which is extremely strong and durable and *Beadalon* ® which is soft, supple beading wire that will hold most beads and most sizes can be easily knotted. Lengths and sizes of cord may vary with the manufacturer and retailer. Use these lists as an approximate.

Nylon Bead Cord is a tight twisted cord that comes on spools or on cards. Carded nylon comes with 6.5 feet (2.5 meters) of thread with an attached twisted wire needle. The cord is strong and durable and beads tend to hang naturally. Nylon cord is easily knotted, and tends to be slightly stronger than silk bead cord. However it does have the possibility of fraying, may stretch over time and is not strong enough for very heavy beads. It comes in a wide variety of colors and the following sizes on cards:

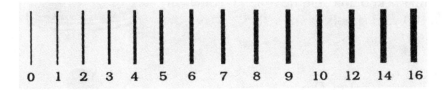

Nylon bead cord also comes in bulk on spools in sizes A (1), D (2), and E (4). They are often sold in 100 yards.

Silk Bead Cord is very similar to nylon but has been traditionally used to string and knot pearls. It is less resistant to rot and decay than nylon cord but tends to stretch less. Silk bead cord also comes on spools in sizes #2 (E) fine, #4 (F) medium, #6 (FF) medium heavy, # 8 (FFF) heavy, or on cards with needles in the same sizes as nylon bead cord.

Beadalon ® is soft, supple beading wire made out of miniature stainless steel wires that are coated in nylon. They come in sizes 7, 19, and 49 in clear, black, gold, blue and white. The sizes indicate the amount of wires coated. Sizes 19 and 49 can be knotted and resist kinks unless extremely abused. Use crimp beads with *Beadalon.* ®

Nymo Bead Thread is a very thin delicate thread used when stitching or weaving seed beads with English beading needles. Sizes range from #AA (200 yards) to #D 400 yards in white. Or sizes 000, 00, and 0, (0 being the thickest. (Not intended for heavy beads). Comes in white or black.

C-Thru Bead Cord is a new soft and strong translucent braided filament cord that is knotable and flexible. It comes in 100 yard spools in sizes .015", .019", .027" and .032".

Bonded Nylon Thread is heat set, stretches little and can be used like nylon or silk cord.

Leather Cord comes in 1/2 mm, 1mm and 2mm diameter , in a variety of colors and is used for beads that are too large for regular bead cord. It is ideal for large clay, wood or carved stone beads.

Genya Cord is made out of artificial leather that comes in 1mm or 2mm in brown, tan, off-white, black and gray.

Rattail Satin Cord comes in 1mm and 2mm widths. Ideal for large stones, wooden and ceramic beads and comes in single strand or braided designs.

Soutache is flat bead cord used like rattail to accentuate large beads and pendants.

Hemp Cord is the alternative cord for use with large wooden and clay beads for weaving and knotting. It comes in 340 yard spools of .5mm cord. Metal clasps are not usually used with hemp cord. The preferred way is by making a knotted loop with one end of the twine and hooking it over a bead at the other end.

Memory Wire is beading wire which is preformed and does not require a clasp. It is extremely difficult to bend so make sure to use industrial strength pliers.

Materials and Tools
Wire

Wire comes in different sizes, shapes and metals. You may wish to begin practicing your techniques with wire made out of base metal and then graduate on to sterling silver (SS), gold filled (GF) and 14k. Base metal wire is generally sold on spools in both gold and silver color while precious metals are sold by the foot or ounce. For the wrapped wire looping technique you will want to use 20-26 Ga. wire. Anything thicker will be too difficult to bend.

Wire is sized in gauges. The lower the number, the thicker the wire:

Ga.	Square	Ga.	Half Round	Ga.	Round
				8	
14		6		10	
16				12	
18		8		14	
20				16	
22		10		17	
24				18	
26		12		20	
28				22	
30		14		24	

We recommend you use round wire for the wrapped wire loop and square wire for wire wrapping stones. Square wire will grip stones and cabochons better than round and can lie flat. Base metal is most commonly found in round gauge while precious metals come in a variety of gauges and shapes.

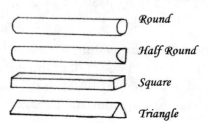

Round

Half Round

Square

Triangle

Materials and Tools
Assorted Findings

There are thousands of different kinds of findings. Here are a few popular ones that were used in this book:

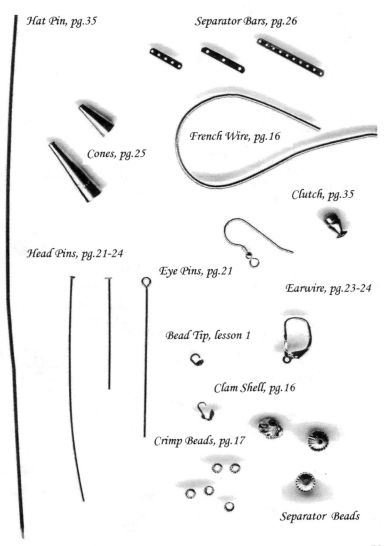

Hat Pin, pg.35

Separator Bars, pg.26

French Wire, pg.16

Cones, pg.25

Clutch, pg.35

Head Pins, pg.21-24

Eye Pins, pg.21

Earwire, pg.23-24

Bead Tip, lesson 1

Clam Shell, pg.16

Crimp Beads, pg.17

Separator Beads

Materials and Tools
Popular and Useful Clasps

Swivel Clasp
(Good for attachments)

Clasp to
glue on
leather

Jump Ring

Hook and Eye Clasps

Lobster Clasps

Toggle Clasps

Interlocking Heart Clasp

Spring Ring

Victorian Clasp

Bead Clasp

Fish Hook Clasp

Multistrand Clasp

54

Materials and Tools
Chain

Sterling silver (SS) and gold filled (GF) chain come in pre-made lengths or in bulk in a wide variety of link styles. Certain links are more conducive than others for attaching wrapped wire loops, eye pins and dangles. Choose styles with large links that will accommodate your loops. Chains with a more identifiable pattern are useful when designing and centering your pieces.

Large Figaro	
Diamond Cut Figaro	
Medium Figaro	
Fine Figaro	
Large Cable	
Flat Link	
Cable	
Large Long and Short	
Medium Long and Short	
Small Long and Short	
Twisted Figure Eight	
Fancy Long and Short	
Figure Eight	
Fancy Cable	

Materials and Tools
Pliers

Chain Nose Pliers are ideal for wire wrapping, crimping, opening jumprings and closing bead tips. They are used throughout this book.

Round Nose Pliers are used for making loops and filigree. Do not use them for gripping because they have a tendency to dent soft wire.

Crimping Pliers are designed especially for crimp beads! They cinch a smooth crimp without unsightly sharp edges.

Bent Chain Nose Pliers are useful for gripping cord in small crevices.

Coil Pliers are designed to make loops and coils without nicking precious wire. Hold the wire with the flat jaw while rotating the round jaw to form a loop. Good for wire wrapped loops! (See pg. 22.)

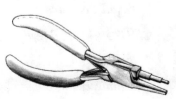

Materials and Tools
Cutters, etc.

Thread Cutters should be well tempered with very sharp edges. Dull blades or scissors have a tendency to cause thread to fray and unravel.

Bead Cord Cutters are ideal for cutting close and completely flush (smooth). Use them on bead cord and very soft wire.

Wire Side Cutters are inexpensive and will cut wire but not flush. They will leave a pointy, rough edge that will need to be filed down.

Flush Wire Cutters are ideal for cutting 20-26 Ga. wire. They will cut a smooth (flush) end that should not snag or scratch.

Knotting Tweezers have extra sharp points and slender shanks which make them invaluable for tying and untying knots.

Beading Awls are used by some beaders to knot close to beads and to untie stubborn knots.

Materials and Tools
Glues and Cement

Using the right kind of adhesive allows you to secure any knot you make. Choose an adhesive which is clear, permanent, quick drying, and does not run. You may need to use a toothpick to apply your glue so that it does not run or glop. There are many different types of adhesives to choose from:

Ideally you will want to choose an adhesive that has a precision applicator such as the **cement** used for watch repair.

A thick **gel**, no drip glue such as cyanoacrylate ester (Super Glue) is also great for bead stringing. Gels don't spill or flow so they prevent the unintentional gluing of beads together or the thickening of bead cord causing it to become brittle.

Epoxies, which are generally used to bond gem materials to metal findings may be applied to end knots however they require mixing and a couple of hours to harden.

Craft cements will work, however with time they may yellow your cord, and may be visible after drying.

White glues are acceptable but not always permanent.

Fabric glues are also useful because they dry clear and flexible and will not harden the cord.

Lastly some beaders use clear **nailpolish** to secure their knots. Nail polish has a useful applicator but is not designed to hold permanently.

Bead Fillers

If you find that some of your bead holes are too large and move on the strand, cut a small piece of bead cord and place a few drops of clear drying glue on it. Stuff the wet glued cord into the bead hole and allow to dry. Do take care not to clog the hole with too much glue.

Materials and Tools
To Further Assist You

A Bead Board is useful for laying out and designing necklaces and bracelets. They come in hard wood finish, velvet or molded plastic with curved grooves and bead storage compartments. Many come with rulers which you can use to measure your necklaces.

A Pin Vise is used to twist wire and augment the appearance of wire wrapped stones. They also hold drills to enlarge bead holes.

A Diamond Reamer is a hand held tool which has several diamond points that are used to enlarge and clean bead holes.

Magnifiers allow the unrestricted use of both hands and help reduce eye strain when working with small beads and intricate designs. Some magnifiers can clip onto eyeglass frames.

A Bead Cord Knotter is a useful tool which mimics the knotting process and saves time. Some beaders find it very helpful.

Appendix 1
Necklace Lengths

Choker (16 inches)

Approximate # of Beads Required:

4mm	100	10mm	40
6mm	68		
8mm	50		

Princess (18-20 inches)

Approximate # of Beads Required:

4mm	112	10mm	45
6mm	76		
8mm	56		

Matinee (23-27 inches)

Approximate # of Beads Required:

4mm	153	10mm	61
6mm	100		
8mm	76		

Opera (35-37 inches)

Women's Bracelet (7 inches)

Men's Bracelet (9 inches)

Anklet (10 inches)

Appendix 2
Bead Sizes

Use the following charts as guidance. Beads are usually measured in millimeters (mm). A size 11 seed bead is approximately the same width as a 2mm bead.

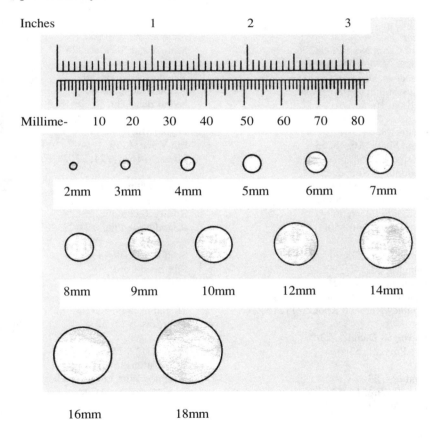

When you knot, make sure to add two to three inches to the length of beads loosely strung on temporary string in order to gauge the finished length. 14 inches loosely strung will equal 16 inches knotted. Add only one inch for a bracelet.

Index